Pearson Education Limited
Edinburgh Gate, Harlow,
Essex CM20 2JE, England
and Associated Companies throughout the world.

ISBN 0 582 41826 7

First published in Great Britain by Michael Joseph 1995
This adaptation first published by Penguin Books 1997
Published by Addison Wesley Longman Limited and Penguin Books Ltd. 1998
New edition first published 1999

Text copyright © Robin Waterfield 1997
Photography copyright © The Baywatch Production Company 1997
All rights reserved

The moral right of the adapter and of the photographer has been asserted

Set in 11/13pt Monotype Bembo by
Rowland Phototypesetting Ltd,
Bury St Edmunds, Suffolk
Printed in Spain by Mateu Cromo, S.A. Pinto (Madrid)

Published by Pearson Education Limited in association with
Penguin Books Ltd., both companies being subsidiaries of Pearson Plc

Contents

Introduction

'The beach is for holidays, Mitch,' Gayle said, 'not for a job.'

'But I save people's lives,' Mitch said. 'What's more important than that?'

'Do you want to save our *lives together?' said Gayle. 'You must decide: do you want me or do you want your job?'*

Mitch Buchannon wants the job. In this book you will find stories about all the other people from *Baywatch*. They want the same job, too. They all want to be lifeguards on the beaches in California. You can find out all about them. Who are Mitch's best friends? Why does Stephanie get angry with CJ? What does Hobie like to do best? Why does Matt leave *Baywatch*? How dangerous is the work of a lifeguard? Here you can read all their secrets.

The first *Baywatch* was on television in 1990. People liked it very much but NBC, the television company, stopped it after one year. It was too expensive, they said. So David Hasselhoff, the actor, and three other people decided to make more stories without the television company's help. *Baywatch* is now world-famous and David Hasselhoff is one of the most famous television actors in the world. *Baywatch* made Pamela Anderson (CJ) world-famous, too. She was in the film *Barb Wire* in 1996.

Deborah Schwartz, the writer, lives in America. She played on the California beaches when she was young. Later, her brother was a lifeguard and the other lifeguards were her friends. She started to write *Baywatch* stories and films in 1991. This is her first book.

The men of *Baywatch*

Mitch Buchannon, the best of them all

Hobie Buchannon, Mitch's son

Logan Fowler, Caroline's boyfriend

Cody Madison, a good swimmer

Matt Brody, CJ's boyfriend

Jimmy Slade, Summer's first boyfriend

Garner Ellerbee, a policeman

Ben Edwards, an older lifeguard

Eddie Kramer, Shauni's husband

John D Cort, CJ's boyfriend

The women of *Baywatch*

Stephanie Holden, Mitch's friend and lover

Caroline Holden, Stephanie's sister

CJ Parker, Matt's girlfriend

Neely Capshaw, pretty . . . but bad

Summer Quinn, Matt's first girlfriend

Shauni McClain, Eddie's wife

Chapter 1 *Baywatch* on TV

Baywatch started in America in 1988. Now 1 billion people in 142 countries watch *Baywatch* on television every week. It is about the lifeguards of south California. *Baywatch* has exciting stories, beautiful people, and good music. It shows the sun, the sea and the beaches of south California. *Baywatch* is not real, it is about the California of Hollywood films, but it has stories about real problems: about being very old or ill, or about being different from other people, and about saving people from the sea. All the family can watch *Baywatch* and find something interesting.

David Hasselhoff – Mitch Buchannon in *Baywatch* – and Pamela Anderson – CJ Parker – are the most famous actors in *Baywatch*.

Chapter 2 Mitch Buchannon

The most important things to Mitch are his son, Hobie, and his work. Mitch is the lieutenant of the Baywatch lifeguards. But when he is in his lieutenant's office, and not out on the beach, he isn't very happy. He wants to be out on the beach all the time; he wants to swim in the sea; he wants to be a real lifeguard. He doesn't want to work in an office.

Mitch loved his wife Gayle. But she didn't like his work. 'It isn't a real job,' she thought. She wanted to have a lot of money and to go to good restaurants and meet rich people. 'The beach is for holidays, Mitch,' she said, 'not for a job.'

'But I save people's lives,' Mitch said. 'What's more important than that?'

'Do you want to save *our* lives together?' said Gayle. 'You must decide: do you want me or do you want your job?'

It was not easy for Mitch. When Gayle moved to Ohio, he decided to stay in Los Angeles. She wanted their young son,

Mitch Buchannon

Hobie, to live with her; she didn't want him to be a lifeguard too.

But Hobie loved his father and wanted to be with him. 'OK,' Gayle told Mitch, 'I understand that Hobie wants to stay here in Los Angeles. I won't take Hobie with me to Ohio. He can live with you.'

Mitch knew that he loved Gayle. Years later he nearly decided to get together with her again, but when Gayle was in the church, a fire started in a fishing-boat at sea. Mitch decided to go and save the people on the boat. Gayle thought, 'For Mitch, work is always going to be more important than me.' So she left him.

Mitch's father was always angry with Mitch too. 'Why do you want to be a lifeguard?' he said. He never stopped being angry with Mitch – and then he died. Mitch's mother only wanted Mitch to be happy, but now his mother is going to die too.

The most important thing for Mitch is his son, Hobie – but there are women too. There's Gayle, and there's Stephanie Holden too. Sometimes, when he saves a woman, she thinks that she loves him, and she runs after him. Sometimes she catches him . . .

But then Mitch met the beautiful Australian, Tracy. She was a lifeguard too. With Tracy, Mitch learnt about real love. He wanted her to be his wife, but she said no. Mitch didn't understand, but then she told him, 'I do not have very long to live.' They went to a beautiful place by the sea. Mitch put his arms round Tracy and she quietly left this world.

Mitch is very brave. More than one thousand people are living because of him. He is often in danger. Some years ago he saved a man from twenty-five metres below the sea, and he nearly died because he swam back up again too fast.

One day he had an accident in the sea and broke his back. He remembered his best friend, Eric Turner. Eric broke his back years ago and could never walk again. 'I helped him to stop being sorry,' Mitch thought, 'but now the same thing is happening to me. Perhaps I won't walk again.' He was in hospital for a long time, but he was very brave and he learnt to use his legs again. Near the hospital, some men with guns were after a young boy. They wanted to kill him. 'I *must* use my legs,' said Mitch. 'I must save that boy.' He stood up, and started to walk – and then to run. He saved the boy, and soon he could swim again.

Mitch's two best women friends are Stephanie Holden and CJ Parker. Perhaps one day he will decide between them. But for now he loves the two of them.

CJ is one of Mitch's oldest friends. When CJ learnt to be a lifeguard, Mitch was her big brother. He helped her when she made mistakes and when she loved the wrong men. When CJ and Cort stopped being lovers, it was very difficult for Mitch because he liked CJ *and* he liked Cort. It was hard for Mitch too when CJ told him her secret, when she came back from France. 'I want to kiss her,' he thought. 'I want to be her lover. I don't want to be her big brother.'

Without Mitch Buchannon there is no Baywatch. He *is* Baywatch. He doesn't *say* he is a better lifeguard than the others, but he is. All the lifeguards like Mitch, and listen to him. When their lieutenant tells them to do something, they do it. They know that he knows best.

Chapter 3   Hobie Buchannon

'Wow! Is your dad really Mitch Buchannon?'

'Yeah.'

'You're lucky! You're on the beach all the time. Your dad has his office on the beach!'

'Yeah, but it's not all swimming and games. I go to school. I have the same problems with my mum and dad that any child has. My mum lives in Ohio and I never see her. But I like living with my dad. I really love him, you know?'

When Gayle came to California to visit Hobie, she brought her rich new boyfriend, Ken. They planned to fly to Mexico for a holiday. 'When Ken and I are husband and wife,' she told Hobie,

4

Hobie Buchannon with Mitch

'I want you to live with us.' But Ken's aeroplane suddenly went down into the water. Hobie saved his mother, but Ken was too afraid to do anything. Mitch saved them all from the sea, but Hobie and Mitch never told Gayle the truth about Ken – that he was afraid.

'I can see that you really love your dad,' Gayle said to Hobie, 'and that you want to live with him. I don't want to lose you, but your dad is important to you. You can live with him, not with Ken and me.' Later, she left Ken.

Some years ago, there was an earthquake in California, and Hobie decided to move to Ohio to live with his mother. But before long he came back to California. Now he's a young lifeguard. He and other young people are learning the job.

Not long ago, Hobie met Lauren. She was a young lifeguard too. Hobie started to love her. But she wasn't well, and Hobie didn't know it. 'Have a nice swim!' Hobie said to her one day.

5

'Yeah!' she said . . . but then she was too weak to come back. Hobie saved her, but her mother and father took her away. 'It's too dangerous for you here,' they told her.

The most important thing for Hobie is his music. Mitch's father never wanted him to be a lifeguard, but Mitch helps *his* son, Hobie, with his music. Hobie has a lot of friends, and now some girlfriends too. But his best friend is always his father. 'Mum moved away six years ago now, Dad,' he says. 'You're really my father *and* my mother. I love you, and I'm always going to tell you the truth.'

'Sometimes that isn't easy,' says Mitch. 'But I'll always tell you the truth too. OK?

'OK,' says Hobie, happily. 'You know, Dad, when I was young, I followed the others. Do you remember that man who was always drunk? I thought he was OK, but I soon saw that he wasn't. Now others are starting to follow me. They listen to me, and people listen to you too. I really am your son!'

Chapter 4   Not Only a Day at the Beach

The sun comes up, there are not many people on the beach, but later more and more people come. There are surfers, and families with children. They play games, talk with their friends, or swim in the sea. The surfers, and the people with boats, go far out to sea. Fifty-nine million people come to the beaches of south California every year.

The lifeguards are on the beach, too. They are there to help all these people. Lifeguarding is a difficult and dangerous job, but lifeguards love to help people.

Scott Hubbell, a real lifeguard for twenty years, helps to make *Baywatch*. He says: 'I like the sea and I want to be near it, and I like saving people at the beach, too. It's very good.'

Tom Zahn is now sixty years old, and saved people at the beach 1,600 times. He says, 'This is the best job in the world.'

Lifeguarding is a difficult and dangerous job,
but lifeguards love to help people

Lifeguards save more people than the police and firemen. In 1994, fifty-nine million people came to the beaches of south California, but only three people died in the sea.

There is a lifeguard school in south California. You must swim 1,000 metres and finish in the first fifty people, and then you can go to this school. At the school, you must swim and run many kilometres every day. You learn to save people and to drive cars on the beach. Most importantly, you learn to stop problems before they start.

Women only started to be lifeguards in 1972. Today there are only thirty-eight women out of the hundreds of lifeguards in south California.

Stephanie Holden with Mitch

Chapter 5 Stephanie Holden

'I want the new lieutenant to be here,' said Mitch — and then she arrived. She was beautiful Stephanie Holden.

'What are you doing here?' asked Mitch, when he went into his office one day and saw her there.

'I'm the new lieutenant,' Stephanie answered.

'But . . . but . . .' said Mitch. He couldn't find the right words.

'I know. Four years ago we were lovers. Is it going to be hard for us to work together?'

'We'll see,' Mitch said. 'But why did you leave me four years ago? I never understood it. What happened? What's your secret?'

'I had a husband,' she answered. 'I didn't like him, but I wanted to try to live with him. So I left you and moved back to him. But things got worse. Now I never see him.'

Before long Mitch and Stephanie were the best of friends again. She was there when Mitch broke his back. And when a man with a gun hurt her and she fell off a ship, Mitch jumped in after her and saved her. After some days together in the sea they were nearly in love again.

Stephanie wants to be the best in everything. She is very young for a woman lieutenant, and she wants to be the boss of all the lifeguards. Often people don't like her, but they are afraid of her. When she tells them to do something, they do it! She can be hard. When Matt Brody was a student lifeguard, she was hard with him and he left the lifeguard school for a few weeks — but then he came back and showed her that he was the best student there.

Stephanie nearly swam in the Olympic Games, but she couldn't, because she hurt her leg. When Cody Madison first arrived in Los Angeles to work as a lifeguard, Stephanie watched him in the sea. 'You're really a very good swimmer,' she said. 'I think you could swim in the Olympics. I'm going to try to help you to be a better swimmer.' Now they work together at his swimming.

CJ Parker and Stephanie live together in a flat. This isn't easy for Stephanie. She likes to put everything away in cupboards, and she likes the house to be clean, but CJ isn't careful: she leaves her shoes and cups and things on the floor! So one day Stephanie got angry with CJ . . . but soon they were good friends again. When Caroline, Stephanie's sister, came to Los Angeles, she moved into the same flat too.

The most important lover for Stephanie was Riley, a man she met after the earthquake in Los Angeles. Riley wanted Stephanie to go away with him round the world on his boat.

'Stephanie won't go away with Riley,' people said. 'She's too careful.' But she did go away with him – for six weeks. But it was only a holiday. Then she came back to her job.

Now Stephanie wants children. But who does she want the father to be?

Chapter 6   CJ Parker

Mitch and Hobie went out on the river for a holiday, and there Mitch met CJ Parker again. 'Some years ago,' Mitch told Hobie, 'CJ was a lifeguard – and a very good one. But she followed her boyfriend to work on the river.'

'But that boyfriend of mine was no good,' said CJ. 'Why do I always get the wrong man? I'm the same as my mother. She always liked the wrong men too.'

'Perhaps you can come back,' said Mitch. 'You can be a lifeguard again.'

CJ was very excited. 'OK, I'll try,' she said. 'But what about the test? I must take it again.'

'You'll be OK,' said Mitch. And she was. She did very well in the test, and started work as a lifeguard again.

She moved into a new flat – and found Stephanie there. 'What are you doing here? This is *my* flat,' Stephanie said.

'No, it's not, it's *my* flat,' said CJ. 'I paid good money for it.'

CJ Parker

'I did too.'

The two girls decided to live together, but they're very different people. CJ often gets angry with Stephanie, and Stephanie gets angry with CJ.

CJ makes many mistakes, but Mitch is always there for her. He's there when she finds that she's in love with the wrong man again, when the earthquake hits Los Angeles . . . and when Cort leaves her.

Before long CJ and Stephanie were good friends. But it was difficult when Caroline, Stephanie's sister, came to live with them too. She and CJ both liked Matt, but he liked CJ, and soon they were lovers.

Matt and CJ were happy together – but then Cort came back. He wanted CJ back. Cort was CJ's boyfriend some years ago, before Matt came to Los Angeles. 'Matt and Cort are the two men in my life,' she thought. 'I love them, but I must decide between them.'

'Why do you want to be with Cort?' Matt asked. 'You and I have a good thing together. Stay with me.'

'I must help him,' CJ answered. 'His eyes are getting weaker and weaker. Soon he won't see anything.'

CJ thought about things for a long time, and then she decided to stay with Matt. They took a holiday together in Hawaii. They had a really good time.

Back in Los Angeles, Matt saved Greta, a beautiful girl from Holland. Greta followed Matt round the place and wanted to do everything for him. CJ wanted Greta to leave. She made a plan. 'Greta follows Matt round,' she thought, 'because he saved her. She must save him too, then she'll stop following him, and she'll go away.' CJ could not find a good plan – but then Greta really *did* save Matt!

When her friend Sadie wanted to be a singer, CJ took her to meet the famous singer Jesse Lee Harris, and soon Sadie started working with Jesse. And CJ and Mitch helped Jesse to go back to his wife and son.

CJ stays with her man through the bad times too. Matt must leave Baywatch. 'This is all because Neely Capshaw says that she cannot work with Matt,' CJ thought. 'Neely says he tried to kiss her, but I know the truth. Neely told me: Matt did not really try to kiss her.' But it was no good. Matt went away to France – and CJ went with him.

When she came back, without Matt, Mitch helped her to forget him and to learn to laugh again. When she told Mitch an important secret, they stopped being friends – and started to be something more than friends!

Chapter 7   Caroline Holden

'You didn't tell me,' said Stephanie. 'Why did you come to Los Angeles?'

'I left my husband,' answered her sister Caroline. 'I can't live with him. He sees other women. Please can I stay with you? I came here to be a lifeguard. I'm a good swimmer.'

Caroline Holden

'I know you're good,' Stephanie said. 'You learnt swimming from me. Will you work hard for the test?'

'Yes, I will,' said Caroline.

On the first night she was in Los Angeles, a big earthquake hit the city. Stephanie was in danger, but Caroline bravely saved her.

Caroline liked tall, dark-haired Matt Brody, but she liked Logan Fowler too. Logan was a student in lifeguard school with her.

'I don't think I can do well in the test,' she told him.

'But your sister is the lieutenant,' Logan said. 'So you'll do well.'

'*I* will swim in the test, not my sister,' Caroline answered. 'She can't swim for me.'

Caroline did very well in the test, and she started work at the beach. Stephanie liked Matt a lot, but she didn't like Logan. 'I'm going to stop seeing Matt,' Caroline told her. 'I want to see only Logan.'

Stephanie got angry with her. 'You're making a bad mistake,' she said.

'Stop telling me what to do,' Caroline said. 'I can decide about my own men. You're my big sister, but why do you think you can decide for me? You can't find the right man for *you*! Your husband was no good.'

Then one day Caroline learnt the truth about Logan. 'Behind my back he's seeing an older woman called Kathleen – a beautiful rich woman,' she thought. She was really angry. 'I can't work on the same beach with him after this.'

But Mitch put them together on the same beach. Things started to go wrong. Sometimes Caroline watched Logan. 'There he is,' she thought. 'He's talking to other women again. Oh no, I mustn't do this. I must always watch the water. A lifeguard always watches the water.' But her eyes went back to Logan – and then she didn't see a child in danger in the sea.

'I'm sorry, Stephanie,' Caroline said later. 'You were right about Logan. He's no good.' But later Logan smiled at her again, and she found him back in her arms.

One day on the beach a man ran over to Caroline. 'My daughter went down in the sea near you,' he said angrily. 'Why didn't you see her? Why didn't you save her? Why? Why?' Caroline looked and looked, but she couldn't find his dead daughter. She talked to everyone about it. 'Oh no,' someone said. 'Don't be sad. That man lost his daughter a year ago.'

Then one day she found a Chinese woman in a small boat on the sea. The woman came from China in the boat because she wanted to live in America. Caroline helped her to find a home and a job.

On holiday in Hawaii, Logan asked Caroline to be his wife. She was very happy – but then she learnt about Logan and his other women. 'No,' she said, 'I won't be your wife. Why do you see other women? You don't really love me.' Back in Los Angeles, a new lifeguard called Cody Madison listened to her and tried to help her to stop crying about Logan.

Chapter 8   Real *Baywatch* Lifeguards

Michael Newman and Gregory Bonann are real lifeguards and they work on *Baywatch*. Gregory Bonann helps to make *Baywatch*. One day he took some writers to the beach, and there he showed them the work of a lifeguard. That day a boy went under the water and Gregory Bonann saved him. The boy was under water for seven minutes, but Gregory saved him. Then the boy went to hospital and after some time he was better.

Michael Newman is an actor in *Baywatch*. He is a lifeguard – and a fireman, too. Michael says, 'My first day on the beach was twenty years ago. I was a new lifeguard, and it was my worst day. I saw all those people on the beach, and I was the only lifeguard for a kilometre. I was really afraid.'

Chapter 9   Logan Fowler

Strong Australian Logan Fowler came to Baywatch at the same time as a big earthquake hit California. He wanted to be a lifeguard in California.

'But you must take the American test first,' said Mitch.

'But I was a lifeguard in Australia,' said Logan. 'I don't want to take the test.'

'All lifeguards here take this test,' Mitch said. 'Do you want to be a lifeguard here?'

'Yes.'

'Then go to school and take the test.'

When the earthquake hit the city, Logan saved a lot of people. 'Now you can see that I'm a good lifeguard,' he told Mitch.

'Yes,' answered Mitch, 'you're right. You *are* a good lifeguard. You showed us that when the earthquake hit. Now show us when you take the test.'

Stephanie didn't like Logan. 'I know that he's brave, and good

Logan Fowler

at his job,' she told her sister, Caroline, 'but I don't like him and I don't want you to like him.'

Then one day Matt got angry with Logan about Caroline, and the two men had a fight. Stephanie wanted them to learn to work together. She put them in a boat together out at sea. 'They *must* work together or the wind will take them away,' she thought. They worked together to save two boys too, but Stephanie wasn't happy with Logan. She wanted him to leave Baywatch.

'I know,' Stephanie thinks. 'It's difficult for Caroline to work on the same beach as Logan, so I'll send Logan to a different beach.'

'You can't do that,' Logan said angrily.

'Yes, I can,' said Stephanie. 'I'm the lieutenant here.'

But Mitch said, 'No, Stephanie, you're wrong. You must say sorry to Logan. I know this will be hard for you to do, but you must do it, and you must bring him back to Baywatch.'

16

Logan liked Caroline a lot, but he wanted to stay in America. 'I must have an American wife,' he thought, 'then I can stay here and work.' So he went after Kathleen, a rich woman from Malibu, and soon Kathleen was his wife. Caroline was very sad, but before long Logan left Kathleen and tried to come back to her.

When Cody Madison arrived, Logan didn't like him much. 'I can see that Caroline likes him,' he thought. 'I don't want her to like him. I want her to like only me. I'll tell people stories about Cody, so they'll think he's a bad lifeguard.'

Only Neely Capshaw understands Logan; she knows his plans.

Chapter 10 Neely Capshaw

When pretty Neely Capshaw came to Baywatch, she went after Matt. 'But I have a girlfriend,' Matt told her. 'I'm not interested in you.'

Neely Capshaw

One day Neely came late to work. 'Why aren't you walking well?' Matt asked. 'Are you drunk? You mustn't come to work drunk. How can a lifeguard do her work when she's drunk?'

'Please don't tell anybody,' Neely said.

But Matt thought, 'I must tell the others. She can't save people when she's drunk. It will be dangerous for them, and for her too.'

Mitch and Matt came to see Neely. 'Were you drunk that day?' Mitch asked.

Neely got angry. 'No, I wasn't,' she said. 'Matt's angry because he wants me to be his girlfriend. He tried to kiss me. I said no, and pushed him away. So then he tells you I was drunk because I pushed him away.'

Then Matt was really angry. 'That didn't happen!' he said. 'I never tried to kiss you. Tell the truth.'

But Neely was clever. 'I think she's telling the truth,' Stephanie said to Mitch.

'Yes, I think you're right,' Mitch said.

Only CJ knew the truth, because Neely told her. But nobody listened to CJ.

'I'm very sorry, Matt,' Mitch said. 'You're a good lifeguard, but you must leave Baywatch. I can do nothing to help you.'

Only Cody Madison really likes Neely, because he doesn't know anything about her. One day Cody saved her from danger down under the water, and later Neely saved him too. So Cody is her only friend.

Neely knows everybody's secrets. She remembers them, and uses them later, when they can help her. She's a good lifeguard, but will she stop getting drunk?

Chapter 11   Cody Madison

'When I first saw you in the sea,' Stephanie says to Cody Madison, 'I thought, "That man is a really good, strong swimmer".'

Cody Madison

'I know I am,' Cody answered. 'I want to swim in the Olympic Games. I think I can do it.'

'I can help you to swim better,' Stephanie said. 'You're good, but you could be better. Why not? What's stopping you?'

'I don't know,' he answered. 'But when my parents died in an accident, I stopped wanting to be the best.'

'OK,' Stephanie said. 'Together we can do something about that. One day you'll be the best in the world.'

Caroline didn't understand. 'What's my sister doing?' she thought. Stephanie got Cody a job in Baywatch, and helped him to be a faster swimmer.

One day Logan said to Cody, 'You're no good. You don't want to be the best. You stop trying.'

Cody didn't like that. 'You're wrong,' he said. 'I do want to be the best. I do. I want that more than anything in the world.'

Now he works very hard with Stephanie's help. 'I *will* try,' he tells Stephanie. 'I *will* be the best in the Olympics.'

Stephanie doesn't want Cody to do dangerous jobs, but one day he swam far under the water to save a young girl. He was OK – and the girl was OK too. He's going to be a good lifeguard, and he's going to be the best and fastest swimmer at the Olympics!

Chapter 12   So Many Beaches, So Little Time

The men and women on *Baywatch* use many different beaches in California for filming.

First there is Venice State Beach. It is a very exciting place with many different people: writers, film-makers, very rich and very poor people, and lots of visitors from all round the world.

Santa Monica State Beach is very good for surfing and swimming.

People come to Will Rogers State Beach for fishing, running,

The men and women on Baywatch use many different beaches in California for filming

and beach games. There is also a place for 2,000 cars. (Will Rogers was a famous Hollywood actor.)

Malibu Surfride Beach has some of the best sea in California for surfers. Lots of very rich people build big, expensive houses at Malibu. Many famous Hollywood actors have their houses there.

People from all round the world come to these beaches, and sometimes they can see the actors make *Baywatch*.

Chapter 13   Matt Brody

Matt's family moved to Los Angeles from France. Sometimes his father tells him what to do, and at other times he doesn't speak to him for days.

'I don't want you to be a lifeguard,' he told Matt. 'What are you thinking about? How can *you* be a lifeguard? You never finish what you start. You're no good at anything.'

'What can I do?' thought Matt. 'I *know* I can be a good lifeguard. I'm going to show my father. I'll show everybody.'

He was a good swimmer at school, so he took the swimming test. There were a lot of other people too. They all wanted to be lifeguards, but Matt did very well, and he started at the lifeguard school.

At lifeguard school he met Stephanie Holden. 'Here you are going to work hard,' she told all the beginners. 'When I tell you to do something, you do it!'

Stephanie didn't like Matt. She gave him more and harder work to do than the others. And at the same time his father said again and again, 'You're no good. Why are you going to that lifeguard school? You'll never be a good lifeguard.'

So Matt left the lifeguard school. But Mitch knew about problems between a father and a son, and he said to Matt, 'Don't stop. You must try again.' Matt went back to the school.

Matt Brody

Back in the school, Stephanie named Matt 'the best in the year'. This happens to only one student in every year. He or she must be a very good swimmer, but Matt did more. When all the students were on the test swim, Matt stopped to help another student, a girl called Summer Quinn. 'Good!' Stephanie thought. 'So he can work with other people. That's very important for a lifeguard.'

Before long Matt and Summer were in love. 'Will you stay with me always?' Summer asked.

'I don't know,' Matt said. '"Always" is a long time.' Summer decided to leave town and go to a school far away in the east.

Later Matt's father wanted to go back to France. 'Goodbye,' Matt said. 'I'm not coming with you.'

Matt's father was angry. 'OK,' he said. 'You're not going to get any money from me.' And he left for France.

'Now I have no money, and no home,' Matt told Stephanie.

'You can move in with CJ and me,' Stephanie said.

CJ was angry with Stephanie. 'You know I like Matt a lot,' she said. 'When he's living with us, what do you think will happen?'

'You must be careful,' Stephanie said, and Matt moved into their apartment. Matt liked CJ too. They tried not to be in love, but it was no good. Soon they were lovers.

Matt was a very brave lifeguard. He saved a lot of people, and did a lot of very dangerous jobs. Everyone liked him. But then there was the problem with Neely Capshaw. Nobody could save him. CJ knew the truth, but nobody listened to her. Matt loved CJ, but he could not stay in Baywatch, so he went back home to France.

Chapter 14 Summer Quinn

Summer and her mother Jackie drove across the country because Jackie wanted to be a singer. She came to LA to find work. Summer started school in Malibu, but she wanted money too, so she looked for a job. Because she was a good swimmer, she tried the lifeguard swimming test.

Hundreds of people try the test each year, but only twenty-five get into lifeguard school, and only twelve will be lifeguards after the school.

'Help!' Summer said. 'How can I do it?'

'You can only try your best,' her mother said.

Summer did get into lifeguard school, along with Matt Brody. A short time later Matt saved Jackie and Summer from Jackie's boyfriend. 'Thanks,' said Summer. 'He tried to hurt my mother.' After that, Summer and Matt were friends.

Summer and Matt went to lifeguard school together. It was very difficult. There was a test on paper and a lot of very hard swimming. Many of the students left the school, but Matt and Summer did well and they stayed. Then it was time for the last test.

'Do you know about this test?' Matt asked Summer. 'We must run, then swim, then run again – and we must jump ten metres into the sea!'

Summer was too afraid to make the jump. Matt waited and helped her. But by now everybody was out in front of them. Together they swam hard for the finish – and came in the first twelve! So they could be lifeguards. They were very happy, and Summer fell into Matt's arms.

Summer and her mother Jackie are very good friends. Jackie was happy that Summer was a lifeguard, but Summer didn't want Jackie to be a singer.

'What's the problem?' Jackie asked.

'You know the restaurants you sing in?' Summer said. 'My

schoolfriends' mothers and fathers go there. It's not nice for me.'

'It's OK,' Jackie said. 'I have a plan.' She stopped being a singer and bought a beach restaurant. Summer was very happy about that. All the lifeguards helped Jackie to get the beach restaurant ready to open. Jackie called the restaurant 'Jackie's Summer Place'.

'You're a good cook,' everybody said, and all the lifeguards came to her restaurant to eat.

Summer's boyfriend was surfer Jimmy Slade. One day Jimmy tried to save her from a man with a gun, but he got hurt. A little later he left Los Angeles to surf on other beaches.

Matt was secretly in love with Summer, but he liked Jimmy too. 'Is it right for me to try to take my friend's girl when he's out of town?' he thought. But he couldn't stop loving Summer, and soon Summer started to love him too.

Then Jimmy suddenly came back. 'What can I tell you?' Summer said. 'I know I was wrong, but Matt and I are in love. What could we do?'

When Jimmy heard about Matt and Summer, he was angry. Then a short time later he had problems in the sea. He was in danger, but Matt saved him. Jimmy left Los Angeles again. 'I'm never coming back this time,' he said.

Summer loved Matt more and more. When she got sick, Matt helped her through it. When she was suddenly afraid of water, Matt helped her to remember. 'Why are you afraid?' he asked. 'Come on! You must try to remember.'

Then she did remember. 'When I was young,' she said. 'My father . . . he shut me in. There was water . . . it was dark . . . I was afraid.'

But the young lovers couldn't stay together. Summer understood Matt. 'I know you're not ready to stay with me always,' she said. 'And that hurts too much, because I want you always. I'm going back east. I'm going to go to school there.' So she left her mother, her job – and Matt.

Chapter 15   Jimmy Slade

Jimmy Slade is the best surfer in the west of the USA. He left home when he was sixteen years old to live by the sea, because he wanted to be the best surfer in the world. Summer Quinn liked him a lot.

Some surfers don't like others to surf on 'their' beach. They tell the others to stay away, they try to hurt them in the water, and they use knives on their cars. It is the job of a lifeguard to help people in the water *and* on the beach, so Mitch sent Matt Brody to look for some of these bad surfers. Matt met Jimmy Slade on the beach and liked him.

'Will you give me surfing lessons?' Summer asked Jimmy later.

'Yes,' Jimmy answered.

Jimmy started to teach Summer about surfing. She was happy. 'This is really good,' she called out to Jimmy.

But then the same surfers tried to hurt them. Summer didn't understand. 'How can they say that a beach is *their* beach?'

This time Matt and the other lifeguards caught the bad surfers and took them to the police.

'You're new in town, Jimmy,' said Matt, 'but you have a good friend – me!'

Jimmy had his arms round Summer. 'Yes,' he laughed, 'and a pretty girlfriend!'

But later he met a rich girl from Malibu, who wanted to help Jimmy be the best surfer in the world. 'Do you want me to help you?' she asked. 'If you want money, ask me.'

'Yes, please,' Jimmy said, but Summer was not happy. The rich girl was beautiful. 'I think she wants to be Jimmy's lover,' Summer said.

When Summer started to be Matt's girlfriend, Jimmy left Los Angeles. Before long, he was the number one surfer in the world!

*Some surfers do not want other people to surf on their beach
and they have fights*

Chapter 16   The Rules of the Game

In summer, each lifeguard watches about 300 to 400 metres of the
beach. Lifeguards must always watch the sea. They can only talk
to somebody for a very short time, and they always look at the
water, never at the person's face.

Lifeguards have telephones and radios, and they can talk to
other lifeguards, or ask for help.

Lifeguards must be very careful in the sea. People are often very
afraid, and then it is difficult to save them. The sea can be very
strong sometimes and it is important not to lose anybody. The
lifeguard must be very careful of the children on the beach and
watch them when they go into the sea.

A good lifeguard knows all of his beach very well. He knows
how many people are on the beach, he knows the weak people

and the strong people; he knows the weather that day, and he knows that the water is warm or cold.

Sometimes there are problems on the beach. Some surfers do not want other people to surf on their beach and they have fights. Also, some people without homes want to live on the beach. A lifeguard will try to help with these problems, but sometimes he must call the police.

Chapter 17   Garner Ellerbee

Born in the east, Garner moved to California, where the sun is warm. He was not a lifeguard, but a policeman – a lifeguard of the city.

One day he got angry with his lieutenant and hit him, and the lieutenant sent him to be a policeman on the beach. Garner doesn't like the sea, but he was happier by the sea than in the police station with the lieutenant. So he was on the beach every day. He found lost dogs, stopped children fighting, and helped people to have a good time.

On the beach he met Mitch and the other Baywatch lifeguards. He helped them and they helped him.

Mitch is his best friend. 'Look, Garner,' Mitch told him one day. 'You want to get off the beach, right?'

'Yeah, that's right,' Garner says.

'So you must say sorry to your lieutenant.'

'No, I won't do that.'

But later Garner went to his lieutenant and said sorry. The lieutenant gave him the worst job in the office. He put him behind a desk, in the darkest room in the building. He never went out on to the streets. He was not a real policeman. Before long, Garner was angry again. He hit the lieutenant again . . . and the lieutenant sent him back to the beach!

When Garner wanted to stop being a policeman, Mitch helped him to decide about a new job. 'What do you really want to do?'

Mitch asked. 'What job do you secretly want to do, but you never tell anybody?'

'In the past I always wanted to be a detective,' Garner said.

'Then do it!' said Mitch. 'And I'll help you.'

So Garner started work as a detective . . . and Mitch had a second job; he started working as a detective along with Garner.

Chapter 18   Ben Edwards

Ben Edwards began work as a lifeguard in the 1950s. In his first summer, a beautiful woman called Maggie James watched Ben at work. She lived by the beach and worked in the movies. She met him, and got him a job in the movies too. They were lovers, but then she left Los Angeles, and Ben went back to work on the beach.

Thirty years later, Ben saw some workmen in Maggie James's old house. 'Somebody is going to sell the house,' he thought.

He went into the house and looked round . . . and found Maggie! 'What are you doing here?' he asked. 'Is it really you?'

'Yes, it's me,' she said with a smile. 'I'm living in this old house again.'

They talked about the old days. 'Let's meet again tomorrow,' Maggie said.

'Yeah,' said Ben. 'I'll be here.' Before long they were lovers again.

One day, when he went to help somebody in the sea, Ben was hurt. 'Now I must stop being a lifeguard,' he told Mitch. 'My leg is bad and the doctors tell me that I'll never really swim again.' Mitch moved him to a desk in the lifeguard's office. It was hard for Ben to work in an office, and it was hard for Mitch to see Ben there, because Mitch liked Ben a lot. 'I always wanted to be a lifeguard,' Ben says to Mitch, 'so I understand that you always wanted the same thing.'

Ben Edwards

Then later Ben saw a young boy in danger. He jumped twelve metres into the water and saved him. He is and always will be a lifeguard.

Chapter 19   California Gold

There are often games meetings on the beaches for real lifeguards. The lifeguards go swimming or surfing, they go out to sea in boats and they run on the beach. Some of these lifeguard 'games' are very difficult. The lifeguards do many of these games together, perhaps surfing, swimming and boating, and they must finish in fifteen to twenty minutes. Many people come to watch these exciting games. Sometimes there are a million people there!

Chapter 20   Shauni McClain

Shauni's mother and father are very rich. She always wore the nicest dresses, shirts and skirts; she drove the best and most expensive cars; she never heard the word 'no'. But beautiful, yellow-haired Shauni liked to be on the beach with her friends. When she left school, she wanted to be a lifeguard. 'I like to be on the beach,' she thought. 'So somebody can pay me when I'm on the beach. I'll work as a lifeguard.'

Shauni's life was always easy, but lifeguard school was hard. 'It's going to be difficult for me to be a lifeguard,' she thought, 'but I *will* do it. I really want to work as a lifeguard.'

At the school Shauni did well in the tests . . . and she met Eddie Kramer, who was a student at the school at the same time. She liked him a lot.

After school, when she was a real lifeguard, Shauni wanted to get a station* on the beach near her friends, but Mitch didn't want to give her a station. 'You're not ready for it,' he said. Shauni was angry, but Mitch put her with Jill Riley, an older lifeguard. On their first day together, a little girl got into danger.

'Quick! Shauni!' called Jill. 'Go and save that girl!'

'I can't! I can't!' cried Shauni. 'I'm afraid! Help me! What do I do!'

Jill saved the little girl; Shauni watched. With Jill's help, Shauni quickly learnt to be a real lifeguard. 'I'm not going to play games with my friends here on the beach,' she said. 'I'm going to save people.' Now she can forget her rich family and her fast cars; when she's on the beach, she's working.

There were many boyfriends in her life, but Shauni learnt about real love from Eddie Kramer. Her rich mother and father didn't like this boy from Philadelphia.

---

* A lifeguard's station is a small house or a very tall chair on the beach for lifeguards to sit in and watch the swimmers in the sea.

'He has no money,' her mother said. 'You can't live with no money, Shauni.'

'Listen, Shauni,' her father said, 'this boy is not right for you. I'm your father. I know you.'

A short time later Eddie saved Shauni's sister Kim. 'Now do you see?' Shauni told her mother and father. 'Eddie's a good man.'

'No. I'm sorry, but we don't like him,' her mother said. 'He's a good swimmer, but is he a good man?'

Shauni decided to leave home. She went to live with Eddie on his boat. They lived together, and worked together too.

One day a girl watched Eddie at work on the beach. 'Wow!' she thought. 'That guy is really good! I think I'm in love with him. I want him to love me too, but perhaps he thinks I'm too fat. What can I do? I know, I'll stop eating.'

After some days, the girl got weak. When she went for a swim, she got into danger. Shauni saved her.

'You think you have a problem because you're fat,' Shauni said. 'But really I have the same problem.'

'But you're beautiful!' said the girl.

'Yeah, so when people look at me, all they see is a beautiful girl,' Shauni said. 'They don't think, "Who is she inside? Is she clever? Is she interesting?" Do you understand?'

'Yes,' said the girl. 'The outside isn't important. Only the inside is really important.'

Mitch, CJ, Eddie and Shauni went on holiday together to a river. CJ watched Shauni for some time and then said, 'What's the problem, Shauni? Are you sad about something?'

'I must talk to Eddie,' Shauni said.

Later, she found Eddie. 'Eddie,' she said, 'I think I'm going to have a baby; your baby.'

'That's good, Shauni!' said Eddie, happily. 'Will you be my wife?'

'You're asking me that only because I'm going to have your baby,' Shauni said.

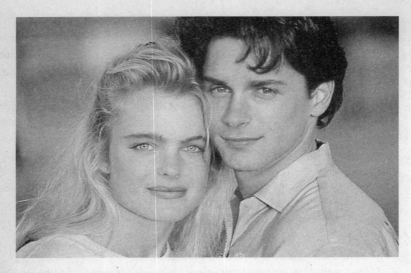

Eddie Kramer and Shauni McClain

But later Eddie saved her from some mountain men. 'I'll always love you,' he said.

Back in Los Angeles, on the beach, Eddie heard the question: 'Do you, Eddie Kramer, take this woman, Shauni McClain, to be your wife?'

'I do,' said Eddie.

Then the happy husband and wife left for Australia. They planned to work over there, and some Australian lifeguards came to California to work in Baywatch.

Chapter 21   Eddie Kramer

Eddie Kramer never knew his father or his mother. The lifeguards and students in lifeguard school in Los Angeles were his first real family. Before long Mitch was his 'father' and Shauni was his girlfriend.

Jimmy, a bad friend from Eddie's past in Philadelphia, came to Los Angeles. He made things difficult for Eddie, and Eddie got into a fight with Jimmy. When Mitch heard about it, he said to Eddie, 'You must leave school for a short time, Eddie. You can come back, but I must show that we don't want fights here.'

But Jimmy didn't stop there. He started a fire in Eddie's lifeguard station – when Eddie and Shauni were inside! Eddie jumped on to the beach from the station with Shauni in his arms!

Later, Eddie met a young girl called Caroline on the beach. Caroline wanted the other girls at school to like her more, so she told them, 'You know Eddie Kramer from the beach? He's my lover.'

When her father heard the story, he was very angry with Eddie. He told the police. 'My daughter is too young to have a lover,' he said. 'That Eddie Kramer is a bad man. Caroline is only a girl.'

Shauni found Caroline, and Caroline told her the truth. 'No, Eddie and I weren't really lovers,' she cried. 'I only wanted people at school to like me.'

'Now you must come and tell the police the truth,' Shauni said. 'Do you want people to think bad things about Eddie? Tell the truth, and Eddie will be OK.'

Eddie loved his brother Bobby, but Bobby wasn't well. He and Shauni visited the hospital. 'This is where Bobby lives,' Eddie said.

'What? All the time?' asked Shauni.

'Yeah.'

Bobby wanted to visit Eddie in Los Angeles. Eddie asked Bobby's doctor about it. 'Yes, that will be OK,' the doctor answered.

But when he was in Los Angeles, Bobby fell into the water. He couldn't swim, but Eddie saved him.

'You know, Shauni,' Eddie said, 'I understand now that it isn't right for Bobby to be out of hospital. I must take Bobby back.'

Shauni kissed him. 'You're right,' she said. 'In the hospital there are doctors to watch him all the time.'

When Shauni was his wife, and he left for Australia, Eddie said, 'One day I'll come back. You guys are my family. I'll be back.'

John Cort with Mitch

Chapter 22   John D Cort

When Mitch left work on ships and started work as a lifeguard, he brought his best friend John Cort with him. But for Cort it was hard to stay in one place for a long time, and soon he left. But later he came back to be a lifeguard again. 'I'm good at this job,' he said, 'and California is the place for me. I like it here.'

Mitch was happy to have him back, but not all the other lifeguards liked Cort. He wanted to put his things in Eddie Kramer's cupboard, because it was his cupboard years ago. 'No,' Eddie says, 'you can't have it. It's *my* cupboard now.' They got into a fight. But Mitch is a real friend, and he loves Cort for better or worse.

Cort had many girlfriends. 'How do you get them?' Mitch asked him one day.

'I don't know,' Cort answered. 'That isn't really important to me, you know.' And he laughed. 'One day I told a woman's dog to jump into the sea. Then I saved the dog and the woman was very happy. She wanted to say thank you, so she gave me a kiss. Soon we were friends . . . but before long I met somebody new!'

But when Cort met CJ Parker, love really hit him for the first time. He left Los Angeles again, but soon came back. He could not leave CJ and he wanted to work as a lifeguard. 'Now I know – I want to be with you,' he told her. 'Now I'll stay with you.'

But one day, after a visit to the doctor, he took CJ by the hand. 'You're sad,' she said. 'What is it?'

'My eyes are slowly going bad,' he said. 'The doctor told me. One day I won't see anything. What am I going to do?'

'Don't be sad,' CJ said. 'I'll always be here for you.'

But Cort thought, 'I must stop being a lifeguard, and I must leave CJ too. It isn't right for me to stay with her. When I can't see anything, I'll only be a problem for her.'

So he said to CJ, 'I'm going to leave Los Angeles.'

'I want to come with you,' CJ quickly said.

But some months later he came back. He learnt about CJ and Matt Brody. 'They're lovers now,' he thought sadly. 'CJ doesn't want me now. She's happy and wants to stay with Matt.'

And so he left again – for the last time.

Chapter 23   Young Lifeguards

Where do lifeguards come from? A lot come from schools. Every summer in south California young people come to the beach and learn how to be a lifeguard. The children must be good swimmers, and then they can come. It is not expensive.

The children come for four hours a day, five days a week for six weeks. They learn about the sea. They learn to swim far out to sea, how to save people, how to jump off a moving boat into the water – everything a real lifeguard does.

ACTIVITIES

Chapters 1–9

Before you read

1 *Baywatch* is about lifeguards. Why do some people want to be lifeguards, do you think? What are the good things about the job, and what are the bad things?

2 Find these words in your dictionary.
    actor   lieutenant   lifeguard   surfer
    Find the second half of each of these sentences
    a   A *lifeguard*   works in a theatre.
    b   A *lieutenant*   plays in the sea.
    c   A *surfer*   is a boss.
    d   An *actor*   works on the beach.

3 Find these words in your dictionary.
    brave   decide   drunk   earthquake   kiss
    real   save   secret   test   together   truth
    Make sentences with the following words.
    a   save / baby / earthquake
    b   secret / tell / truth
    c   brave / drunk / sea
    d   kiss / conversation / together
    e   test / real / decide

After you read

4 Which of these sentences are wrong, and why?
    a   Mitch has problems with his wife and father.
    b   Mitch's wife marries another man.
    c   Mitch's son is a lifeguard.
    d   Everybody likes Stephanie.
    e   CJ loves two men at the same time.
    f   Logan and Cody Madison are good friends.
    g   The two sisters like Logan.
    h   In real life there aren't many women lifeguards.

5 Work with another student. Have the conversation between Caroline and Logan on Hawaii.

Student A: You are Logan. You love Caroline and want to marry her. Don't tell her the truth about the other women in your life. Tell her that you love only her.

Student B: You like Logan, but you don't want to marry him. Tell him that you know about the other women in his life. Tell him that you like the new lifeguard, Cody Madison.

Chapters 10–16

Before you read

6 Find these words in your dictionary:

gold   guy   rule

Which of them go with the following words?

a to break a . . . . .   **b** a . . . . . watch   **c** a happy . . . . .

7 Neely Capshaw is a good lifeguard, but she's often drunk.
Do you think that this is a big problem for a lifeguard?
Why, or why not?

After you read

8 Which chapters do these sentences go with?

a	Put that bottle down!	Cody Madison
b	Matt is telling the truth!	Matt Brody
c	I'm going to be famous one day.	Neely Capshaw
d	My father is the same as yours.	Summer Quinn
e	Don't be afraid.	Jimmy Slade
f	I'm sorry, but I'm in love with your friend.	Neely Capshaw
g	I'm the best in the world!	Summer Quinn

9 Why do these people leave *Baywatch*?

a Matt Brody?   **b** Summer Quinn?   **c** Jimmy Slade?

10 You want to be a lifeguard. One of these people will be your teacher: Matt Brody, Cody Madison, CJ Parker or Stephanie Holden. Which one do you want, and why?

Chapters 17–23

Before you read

11 Find the word *movies* in your dictionary. It means the same as:
    a television **b** film **c** theatre **d** newspapers

12 Sometimes a million people go to the beach and watch the lifeguard 'games'. What games do the lifeguards play, do you think? Why do people like watching them?

After you read

13 Who are these sentences about?
    a He isn't a lifeguard.
    b He is CJ's boyfriend.
    c He worked with Mitch before Mitch was a lifeguard.
    d He worked in movies.
    e He nearly died in a fire.
    f She makes problems for Eddie.
    g He has a bad leg
    h She has rich parents.

14 Why does John Cort leave *Baywatch*? Do you think he is right? Why, or why not?

Writing

15 You are a lifeguard *or* a beach policeman. Write about one exciting day in your life.

16 On Page 12, CJ tells Mitch an important secret. What do you think that secret is? Write a short story about it.

17 You are John Cort. After you leave *Baywatch* for the last time, you write a letter to CJ. Tell her about your new life and about your feelings.

18 Which person in *Baywatch* do you like best, and why? Which person do you hate most, and why? Use the pictures and stories in this book to help you. Write about these two people for a student magazine.